Finding Love in the Rainbow: A Guide to Black Gay Dating

Chapter 1: Embracing Your Identity

In the journey of life, understanding and accepting who you are is pivotal. This is especially true in the context of Black gay dating, where the intersections of race and sexuality present unique challenges and profound opportunities for personal growth.

When you step into the world of dating, it's like opening a new book filled with unknown characters and unfolding stories. For a Black gay individual, this book is not just a tale of seeking companionship but also one of self-discovery and affirmation. The path to true connection begins with a deep appreciation of your own identity.

Understanding and Celebrating Your Black Identity

Your Black identity is rich with history, culture, and power. It is a tapestry woven with the threads of resilience and creativity of generations that came before you. In a world that often tries to paint a monolithic picture of what it means to be Black, it's important to understand the diversity within your community. Celebrate the strength, beauty, and diversity of your Black heritage. Let it be a source of pride as you navigate through the often complex dating scene, where you might encounter stereotypes or prejudices even within your own LGBTQ+ community.

Building Self-Confidence and Self-Acceptance

Self-confidence is your armor against the challenges you will face. It grows from the seeds of self-acceptance. Recognize that you are worthy of love and respect just as you are. This can be a tough journey, as societal pressures and internalized messages of inadequacy can be harsh and persistent. Engage with positive affirmations, seek out role models who reflect the best of what you aspire to be, and surround yourself with a supportive community. Remember, the acceptance of oneself fosters authenticity and attracts people who appreciate the real you.

Embracing Your Sexuality and Finding Your Voice

Your sexuality is an integral part of who you are—it is not a phase or something to be compartmentalized. Embrace it as a core aspect of your identity. In the context of dating, this means being open about your desires and boundaries. Communicate your feelings, fears, and expectations with potential partners without shame. Finding your voice in this space allows you to forge more meaningful and respectful connections. It also serves as a beacon for others who might still be struggling with their acceptance. Navigating the dating world as a Black gay individual is not just about finding someone who complements you. It is also a profound journey of self-empowerment. Every interaction, every setback, and every success teaches you more about yourself and how you relate to others.

As you embark on this journey, carry with you the knowledge that your identity is a beautiful and complex mosaic. Each piece—your heritage, your experiences, your dreams—comes together to create the unique and wonderful person that you are. In embracing your full identity, you not only become a participant in the dating world but also a creator of your narrative, one where you write the rules of love, acceptance, and joy.

Chapter 2: Exploring the Dating Landscape

With a strong sense of identity firmly in place, the next step in your journey is to navigate the exciting and sometimes intimidating world of dating. This chapter will guide you through the varied landscapes where connections blossom: from digital realms of dating apps to vibrant social events.

Delving into the Diverse World of Black Gay Dating Apps and Websites

The digital age has transformed the way we connect, and for the Black gay community, dating apps and websites offer a unique platform to meet potential partners. These platforms cater to a range of preferences and identities, allowing you to filter and find matches that share your values and interests. Popular apps and niche sites for the Black LGBTQ+ community not only facilitate romantic connections but also foster a sense of belonging and understanding.

When exploring these platforms, prioritize safety and honesty. Be clear about what you're looking for, and use features designed to protect your privacy and well-being. Remember, the goal is to enhance your dating experience, providing a gateway to meet others, not a final destination.

Attending Black Gay Bars, Clubs, and Social Events

Physical spaces like bars, clubs, and social gatherings remain vital for the community. These venues offer a sensory experience that apps simply cannot match—the thrill of a first encounter, the sound of laughter, and the dance of eyes meeting across the room. Black gay bars and clubs, often cultural havens, provide safe spaces where you can express yourself freely and celebrate your identity with others who understand your journey.

Moreover, attending LGBTQ+ events such as pride festivals, poetry slams, and cultural showcases can deepen your connection to the community. These events are not only fun but also enriching, offering opportunities to engage with arts, culture, and activism that reflect your experiences and aspirations.
Connecting with Like-Minded Individuals Through Shared Interests and Hobbies
One of the most fulfilling ways to meet new people is through shared interests and hobbies. Whether it's joining a book club, taking a dance class, or volunteering for LGBTQ+ causes, activities that align with your passions provide natural opportunities to meet others who share your enthusiasm. These settings are less pressured than traditional dating scenarios, allowing relationships to grow organically from a

foundation of mutual respect and enjoyment.

Expanding Your Social Circle and Putting Yourself Out There

Expanding your social network is crucial in the dating world. Every new friend or acquaintance brings the potential to introduce you to someone special or to offer new experiences. Be open to making connections beyond immediate romantic interests. Attend meetups, network at community events, and even leverage social media platforms to engage with local and global communities.

Remember, the essence of putting yourself out there is about being proactive and open to life's possibilities. It means stepping out of your comfort zone, embracing vulnerability, and being willing to take risks for the sake of personal growth and connection.

As you explore the rich tapestry of the dating landscape, keep in mind that each experience—whether a moment of connection or a lesson learned—is a stepping stone toward finding what truly fulfills you in a relationship. The journey might be fraught with challenges, but each step forward is a stride toward finding companionship, love, and a deeper understanding of yourself and others.

Chapter 3: Navigating the First Date

The first date can be a thrilling prospect, filled with potential and promise. It's a crucial moment where first impressions are made and the foundation of a potential relationship can begin to take form. This chapter explores how to approach this initial encounter with confidence, respect, and genuine interest.

Breaking the Ice and Making a Good First Impression

The first few moments of a date can set the tone for the entire experience. Start with a warm greeting—smile, make eye contact, and perhaps offer a light, appropriate physical gesture like a handshake or a hug, depending on what feels right for the moment and what you've gauged from their body language. Icebreakers can be simple; comment on a shared interest you discovered through your initial conversations or something timely and positive you've observed around you. Dress appropriately for the occasion, showing that you value the time you both have set aside to meet. Being punctual, presentable, and polite not only respects their time but also shows self-respect and establishes a basis for mutual respect throughout your interaction.

Finding Common Ground and Sparking Meaningful Conversations

To foster a connection, steer the conversation towards topics of shared interest. Discuss favorite hobbies, books, movies, or experiences. These discussions can reveal deeper values and passions, allowing both of you to connect on a meaningful level. Ask open-ended questions to encourage dialogue rather than simple yes or no answers. Listen actively and attentively, showing genuine interest in what they say. This not only helps in understanding the person better but also makes them feel valued and listened to.

Setting Boundaries and Respecting Each Other's Personal Space

An essential aspect of any first date is establishing and respecting personal boundaries. It's important to communicate your boundaries clearly and respectfully. Pay attention to their cues as well—both verbal and nonverbal. This respect for each other's comfort zones not only enhances trust but also helps both parties feel secure and relaxed.

Discuss expectations if the situation calls for it—whether you're looking for something casual or a more serious relationship. Such honesty can prevent misunderstandings and build a trustworthy foundation for whatever type of relationship both of you might pursue.

Assessing Compatibility and Potential for a Long-Term Connection

While it's important not to put too much pressure on a first date, it's also useful to consider signs of compatibility. Do your conversations and interests align? Do your humor and values resonate with each other? Notice if the interaction feels balanced; are both of you contributing to the conversation, or does one dominate? Such dynamics can be indicators of how a relationship might develop.

However, not every moment of silence needs to be filled, and not every difference means incompatibility. Some of the most resilient relationships thrive on the balance between commonalities and differences, each individual bringing something unique to the partnership.

Remember, the goal of a first date is not just to impress, but to express who you are and discover who your date is. Whether or not a first date leads to a second, each meeting is an opportunity to learn more about yourself, what you enjoy, and what you seek in a relationship. Approach each date with openness and curiosity, and let the journey unfold naturally.

Chapter 4: Intimacy and Beyond

Intimacy, in the context of Black gay relationships, encompasses a wide range of experiences and emotions. It is the thread that weaves together physical closeness with emotional depth, fostering a bond that can sustain and enrich a relationship. This chapter delves into the complexities of intimacy, communication, and maintaining a healthy relationship.

Exploring the Complexities of Intimacy in Black Gay Relationships

Intimacy is multifaceted and extends beyond physical interactions; it involves emotional, intellectual, and sometimes spiritual connections. For Black gay couples, the journey towards deep intimacy can be influenced by external pressures such as societal prejudices and internal challenges like prior experiences of discrimination. It's important to acknowledge these unique pressures and work together to create a safe space where vulnerability is not just possible but encouraged. Recognize that intimacy grows over time, developing through shared experiences and trust. It requires patience, understanding, and a conscious effort from both partners to continuously engage and connect in meaningful ways.

Fostering Open Communication and Mutual Understanding

Effective communication is the cornerstone of any strong relationship. It involves more than just talking about your day; it requires the ability to express your deepest fears, joys, and uncertainties. Open communication in Black gay relationships can help bridge gaps in understanding and build a foundation of trust.

Encourage regular check-ins and be proactive in discussing feelings and expectations. Use 'I' statements to express your thoughts and feelings without making your partner feel defensive. Listen actively, without preparing your response while your partner is speaking. This fosters a

deeper understanding and shows that you value what they have to say.
Navigating Sexual Health and Safe Sex Practices
Sexual health is a critical aspect of any relationship and is especially important in the LGBTQ+ community, where specific health concerns may be more prevalent. Discussing sexual health openly—including histories, health status, and safe sex practices—should not be taboo. Instead, it should be seen as another layer of caring for each other's well-being.
Stay informed about the latest in safe sex practices and health services available for the LGBTQ+ community. Regular health check-ups, being honest about one's health, and making informed choices about protection methods are all part of maintaining both your health and that of your partner.

Strengthening the Bond and Deepening the Connection
To deepen the bond in your relationship, engage in activities that both partners find fulfilling. Whether it's traveling, cooking, or participating in community service, shared activities can strengthen your connection and create lasting memories.
Emphasize the importance of personal growth within the relationship context. Supporting each other's goals and aspirations can enhance individual satisfaction, which in turn, benefits the relationship.
Finally, make room for appreciation and gratitude. Recognize and celebrate each other's strengths and contributions to the relationship. This not only affirms your partner's value but also reinforces your commitment to each other.

By understanding and navigating these aspects of intimacy, you can build a robust and loving relationship that stands the test of time and enriches every facet of your life.

Chapter 5: Planning for the Future

Planning for the future is an essential part of any committed relationship. It involves setting mutual goals, embracing new experiences together, and building a durable foundation for a fulfilling partnership. This chapter outlines how to effectively plan for a shared future that is rewarding.

Discussing Long-Term Goals and Expectations for the Relationship

Communication about plans not only helps align expectations but also strengthens the bond between partners. It's important to have open discussions about key topics such as career aspirations, financial planning, living arrangements, marriage, and possibly parenting. These conversations should be approached with openness and flexibility, recognizing that individual dreams and goals can evolve.

Approach these discussions with an understanding that compromise is often necessary, but it should not mean sacrificing core values or important personal goals. Instead, find ways to support each other's aspirations while forging a shared path forward.

Exploring Opportunities to Travel and Experience New Things Together

Traveling and experiencing new activities together can significantly strengthen a relationship. It offers a break from routine, presents challenges that you must manage as a team, and provides unique memories that you can look back on. Whether it's a road trip to a nearby city, an international adventure, or trying out a new hobby together, these experiences can foster growth and deepen your connection.

Make it a point to regularly discuss places and experiences you both are interested in. Planning these adventures together can be as rewarding as the experiences themselves.

Building a Strong Foundation for a Lasting and Fulfilling Partnership

A lasting partnership is built on more than love—it requires mutual respect, trust, and understanding. Ensure that your relationship is built on a strong foundation by regularly nurturing these aspects. This can involve:

- Regularly expressing appreciation and affection.
- Actively listening and responding to each other's needs and concerns.
- Maintaining a healthy balance between togetherness and individuality.

Invest in the health of your relationship by periodically reviewing your dynamics and addressing any emerging issues before they become serious problems. Consider activities that strengthen your bond, like relationship workshops or couples counseling, as part of your ongoing commitment to each other.
Embracing the Journey of Love and Companionship
Finally, recognize that the journey of love and companionship is ongoing and dynamic. Embrace the natural ups and downs that come with sharing a life. Celebrate the milestones and achievements along the way, and learn from the challenges as they help you grow both individually and as a couple. Stay committed to nurturing your partnership through all phases of life. By planning for the future, embracing new experiences, and building a strong

foundation, you set the stage for a long and joyful journey together. Let your relationship be a source of stability, joy, and continual growth as you both evolve and navigate the complexities of life side by side.

Author Notes: Tips and Advice for Successful Dating

1. Be Authentic

One of the most fundamental pieces of advice for dating is to be yourself. Authenticity attracts, while pretense can only be maintained for so long. Embrace your quirks, share your true interests, and be honest about your ambitions and desires. Authentic interactions are the foundation of meaningful connections.

2. Communicate Openly and Honestly

Communication is key in any relationship, and it starts from the very first date. Be clear about your intentions and feelings, and encourage your date to do the same. This builds a foundation of trust and mutual respect, which are essential for any potential relationship.

3. Keep Expectations Realistic
While it's natural to daydream about the potential of a new relationship, keeping expectations realistic helps you stay grounded and avoid disappointment. Take the time to get to know the other person and allow the relationship to develop naturally without forcing predefined expectations on it.

4. Practice Active Listening
Show genuine interest in your date by practicing active listening. This means fully concentrating on what is being said rather than just passively hearing the message. Ask questions, reflect on what you've heard, and show empathy. This not only makes your date feel valued but also helps you understand them better.

5. Prioritize Safety
Always prioritize your safety, especially when meeting someone new. Choose public places for initial dates, inform a friend or family member of your plans, and trust your instincts. If something doesn't feel right, don't hesitate to leave the situation.
6. Manage First Date Nerves
It's normal to feel nervous before a first date. Try to manage these nerves by preparing ahead of time, choosing a comfortable setting, and setting realistic expectations for the meeting. Remember, it's just an opportunity to meet someone new and possibly make a connection.
7. Embrace Rejection as Part of the Process
Rejection is an inevitable part of dating but it's not a reflection of your worth. Each rejection is an opportunity to learn and grow. Keep a positive

outlook and don't be discouraged—
every experience is a step closer to
finding someone who is a better match
for you.
8. Enjoy the Journey
Finally, try to enjoy the dating process.
While the goal may be to find a long-
term partner, the experiences along the
way are valuable in themselves. Each
person you meet can teach you
something new, whether about
relationships, the world, or yourself.
Dating is as much about self-discovery
as it is about finding someone else.
Keep these tips in mind, stay true to
yourself, and maintain a positive, open
attitude throughout your dating
adventures.